John Foster and Korky Paul
MONSTER
POEMS

Oxford University Press
Oxford   New York   Toron

Acknowledgements

The editor and publisher are grateful for permission to include the following poems:

Michael Baldwin, 'The Truth about the Abominable Footprint', © 1995 Michael Baldwin. Reprinted by permission of the author.

Paul Cookson, 'It', © 1995 Paul Cookson. Reprinted by permission of the author.

Richard Edwards, 'Three of a Kind', from *The House That Caught a Cold* (Viking, 1991); 'The Sliver-Slurk', from *A Mouse in my Roof* (Orchard Books, 1988); and 'The Last Monster', © 1995 Richard Edwards. All reprinted by permission of the author.

Eric Finney, 'The Night of the Junk Monsters', © 1995 Eric Finney. Reprinted by permission of the author.

John Foster, 'The Snow Monster' and 'The Fire Monster', © 1995 John Foster. Reprinted by permission of the author.

David Harmer, 'Watch Your Teacher Carefully', © 1995 David Harmer. Reprinted by permission of the author.

Julie Holder, 'The Alien' and 'The Monster Behind the Loo', © 1995 Julie Holder. Reprinted by permission of the author.

Robin Mellor, 'The Glamdrak', © 1995 Robin Mellor. Reprinted by permission of the author.

Trevor Millum, 'Tell Me It Isn't', © 1990 Trevor Millum, first published in *The Usborne Book of Creepy Poems*, edited by Heather Amery (1990). Reprinted by permission of the author.

Michaela Morgan, 'Question Time' and 'Be Wary of the Werewolf Wild', © 1995 Michaela Morgan. Reprinted by permission of the author.

Brian Morse, 'Get You', © 1995 Brian Morse. Reprinted by permission of the author.

Brian Moses, 'The Grumposaurus' from *Hippopotamus Dancing* (CUP, 1994). Reprinted by permission of the author, and Cambridge University Press.

Judith Nicholls, 'Make Your Own Monster: A DIY Guide', © 1995 Judith Nicholls. Reprinted by permission of the author.

Jack Prelutsky, 'Help', from *The Snopp on the Sidewalk*, © 1976, 1977 by Jack Prelutsky. Reprinted by permission of Greenwillow Books, a division of William Morrow & Company, Inc. 'The Underwater Wibbles' from *The New Kid on the Block*, © 1984 by Jack Prelutsky (published in the UK by Wm Heinemann and in the USA by Greenwillow). Reprinted by permission of Reed Consumer Books and Greenwillow Books, a division of William Morrow & Company, Inc.

Rowena Sommerville, 'The Monster's Heart', © 1995 Rowena Sommerville. Reprinted by permission of the author.

Clive Webster, 'Mistaken Identity' and 'Epitaph for Frankenstein', © 1995 Clive Webster. Reprinted by permission of the author.

For Paul Hamilton Christie Gordon. K.P.

ENDPAPERS by Joanna Mitchell
(aged 5½ years)

Oxford University Press, Great Clarendon Street, Oxford OX2 6DP

Oxford New York
Athens Auckland Bangkok Bogota Buenos Aires Calcutta
Cape Town Chennei Dar es Salaam Dethi Florence
Hong Kong Istanbul Karachi Kuala Lumpur Madrid
Mclboume Mexico City Mumboi Nairobi Paris
Sao Paxlo Singapore Taipei Tokyo Toronio Warsw

and associated companies in
Berlin Ibadan

Oxford is a trade mark of Oxford University Press

This selection and arrangement © John Foster 1995
Illustrations © Korky Paul 1995

Firt published 1995
Reprinted in paperback 1998

A CIP catalogue record for this book is available from the British Library

ISBN 0 19 276147 1

Printed in Hong Kong

CONTENTS

Question Time

WHAT DOES A MONSTER LOOK LIKE?

Well . . . hairy
and scary,
and furry
and burly and pimply and dimply and warty and naughty and wrinkled and
crinkled . . .
That's what a monster looks like.

HOW DOES A MONSTER MOVE?

It oozes,
it shambles,
it crawls and it ambles, it slouches and shuffles and trudges, it lumbers
and toddles, it creeps and it waddles . . .
That's how a monster moves.

WHERE DOES A MONSTER LIVE?

In garden sheds,
under beds,
in wardrobes, in plug holes and ditches,
beneath city streets, just under your feet . . .
That's where a monster lives.

HOW DOES A MONSTER EAT?

It slurps and it burps and gobbles and gulps and sips and swallows and
scoffs, it nibbles and munches, it chews and it crunches . . .
That's how a monster eats.

WHAT DOES A MONSTER EAT?

Slugs and bats and bugs and rats and stones and mud and bones and blood
and squelchy squids . . . and nosy kids.
YUM!
That's what a monster eats!

Michaela Morgan

It

It hides inside your wardrobe.
It hides beneath your bed.
Sometimes Its eyes are yellow
And sometimes they are red.
It makes those spooky noises
That no one else can hear
And when you're fast asleep
It whispers in your ear.
It has ten thousand teeth
And eats your underwear
And when you try and find your vest
It's never ever there.
It has a great big hairy nose
That's full of boils and spots
But doesn't seem to smell a thing
Because It eats your socks.
It hides your favourite toys
And breaks your favourite game.
It colours on your favourite book
And you get all the blame.
It stops you doing homework
And switches on the telly.
It forces you to eat up all
The chocolate cake and jelly.

Sometimes It's very scary
And sometimes It is not.
Sometimes It makes you very cold
And sometimes very hot.
When Mum and Dad and you
Are at the table to be fed
It makes a nasty noise and smell
And you get sent to bed.
It pinches all the sheets
In the middle of the night.
It makes the curtains flutter
And the bedroom door slam tight.
It taps upon your window.
Its face is on the moon.
It brings to life all shadows
That live inside your room.
It's the last thing you remember
Before you go to sleep.
It nearly bit your toes off.
It nearly ate your feet.
But always when you wake up
And feel the morning sun,
It's never ever there.
It's always always . . . gone.

Paul Cookson

Help

Can anybody tell me, please,
a bit about the thing
with seven legs and furry knees,
four noses and a wing?

Oh, what has prickles on its chin,
what's yellow, green, and blue,
and what has soft and slimy skin?
Oh, tell me, tell me, do.

And tell me, what has polka dots
on every other ear,
what ties its tail in twenty knots,
what weeps a purple tear?

Oh, what is growling long and low
and please, has it been fed?
I think I'd really better know . . .
it's sitting on my head.

Jack Prelutsky

8

Get You

He drew a monster
on the inside cover
of his library book.
That was at bedtime,
but he fell asleep.

By morning
his monster
seemed bigger,
its eyes
more open wide,
its ears more pointed.
A drop of blood
flecked its chin.

By bedtime
that night
it was inching
towards the edge of the paper.
As he quickly closed the book
the monster grinned.

Brian Morse

Tell Me It Isn't!

Try not to stare
But tell me — that shadow there
With its head in the air
It isn't a bear . . .
There *isn't* a bear
Come out of its lair
At the top of the stair
Is there?

Take care how you speak,
But tell me, that creak,
It isn't the creak of the freak
The flying freak
With the crooked beak
About to sneak
Up from behind
IS it?

Tell me, that sound
Isn't the sound of the hound
The red-eyed hound
Creeping around
Dribbling and crunching
The bones it found
About to leap with one bound
On my back! *It isn't, is it?*

Tell me, that movement I saw
Behind the door
It wasn't a paw
Wasn't a claw
It wasn't the Beast
About to roar
And pounce and gnaw —
WAS IT?

Yes, I know you told me before
But I'm still not sure
So, tell me *once* more.

Trevor Millum

10

The Monster Behind the Loo

The Monster behind the loo
Isn't there
Till you sit on the ring of the seat
And just when you're in
The middle of things,
A spider scuttles down the wall
A daddy-long-legs pays a call
A moth flies out of the toilet roll
And the Monster
Scuffles
Its
Feet!

Julie Holder

SHUFFLE
SHUFFLE SHUFFLE
SHUFFLE SHUFFLE
SHUFFLE
SHUFFLE SHUF
SHUFFLE
SHUFFLE SHUFF
SHUFFLE SH
SHUFFLE

The Grumposaurus

Each morning a grumposaurus
tears into our bedroom,
she burrows down
beneath the duvet
and roars out commands
most grumposaurusly:
'Where's my drink?'
'I want a story!'

We really have to take care
not to annoy this beast,
give her milk and cereal,
a TV cartoon or two.
Then at times the grumposaurus
can be quite friendly,
she hugs and smothers us,
tries to mother us . . .

The Alien

The alien
Was as round as the moon.
Five legs he had
And his ears played a tune.
His hair was pink
And his knees were green,
He was the funniest thing I'd seen
As he danced in the door
Of his strange spacecraft,
He looked at me —
And laughed and laughed!

Julie Holder

12

But we never know when
she'll turn grumposaurus,
we never know when,
mouth-wide, she'll roar at us,
or sit in a huff
and just ignore us.
It's a tough life
living with a grumposaurus.

Brian Moses

Mistaken Identity

I thought I'd seen a monster
From Outer Outer Space,
Till Dad said, 'No, it's just your mum
With a mud-pack on her face . . .'

Clive Webster

Make Your Own Monster: A DIY Guide

How do you make a monster?

Not with the glare of a torch-eye
slicing into the dark;
not with a gash of yellow paint
or the swing of a bat-wing cloak.
Nor with the roar of a dinosaur
or a sudden ruler-crack,
nor with egg-boxes, staples, glue . . .

This is what you do . . .

You lie awake after twilight
under a starless sky;
you leave your window just ajar
and feel the night creep by.
When the window squeaks
you start to sweat,
you remember the wind is still
and yet . . .
A creak in the hall
crawls on to the stair
and you know that somehow,
something is there . . .

Your mouth is dry
and the hairs on your back
stand to attention,
stopped in their track.
And a shadow crouches
by the door . . .
gathers breath
then slowly creeps

across the floor

TOWARDS YOU!

Then, you can be sure,
you've made your monster!

Judith Nicholls

The Night of the Junk Monsters

'In the time I've been school caretaker
I've seen many a curious sight,
But nothing so strange, or mad or daft
As what I saw last night.
There were five junk monsters dancing —
The ones made by 4C —
Whooping it up in the school hall.
Scared the daylights out of me!'

'Tell me again, please. And slowly.'

'Well, I'd been down to the pub,
Saw these lights in school on my way home —
Too late for an after-school club.
I looked in through the big hall window
And I nearly had a fit:
That robot thing made of soap powder packs
Going mad on the school drum kit!
The other four laughing and lumbering round
In some sort of dance or chase,
That dangly one with the coat hangers
Seemed to be setting the pace.
And the nasty, blobby, green one,
It's made from some curtains, I think,
Was laughing and heaving and wobbling away
With the snaky one that's pink.
I must have been there at the window
Half an hour with both eyes popping;
I left them at it in the end —
They showed no sign of stopping.'

'Well, I've checked on your midnight monsters,
I've been down to that classroom just,
And they're all safely back in their places,
Lifeless and gathering dust.
It's a really fantastic story . . .'

'Headmaster, it happened that way!'

'Let's go through it just once more:
You'd been down to the pub, you say . . .'

Eric Finney

17

The Monster's Heart

My master made me, chose each part,
then set me living, with a heart,
a hopeful, human heart.

His monstrous skill encased within
an envelope of tortured skin,
the muscles, sinews, bones, the brain
that works my body, knows my pain.
I lurched, I lumbered in the light,
but each one turned from me in fright;
I looked for love, encountered dread,
and learned that I were better dead.
The human world is not a place
to welcome this inhuman face,
so now I hide in bitter shade,
and curse the day that I was made.

I curse my maker and his art,
but most of all, I curse my heart,
my lonely, human heart.

Rowena Sommerville

Epitaph for Frankenstein

When Frankenstein's Monster finally died,
And his reign of terror ceased,
These were the words they inscribed on his grave:
'May the occupant Rust in Peace.'

Clive Webster

Watch Your Teacher Carefully

It happened in school last week
when everything seemed fine
assembly, break, science, and spelling
three twelves are four times nine.

But then I noticed my teacher
scratching the skin from her cheek
a forked tongue flicked from her lips
her nose hooked into a beak.

Her twenty arms grew longer
they ended in terrible claws
by now she was orange and yellow and green
with crunching great teeth in her jaws.

Her twenty eyes were upon me
as I ran from the room for the Head
got to his office, burst through the door
met a bloodsucking alien instead.

Somehow I got to the staffroom
the doorknob was dripping with slime
inside were seven hideous things
who thought I was dinner time.

I made my escape through a window
just then a roaring sound
knocked me over flat on my face
as the whole school left the ground.

Powerful rockets pushed it
back into darkest space
all I have left are the nightmares
and these feathers that grow on my face.

David Harmer

The Underwater Wibbles

The Underwater Wibbles
dine exclusively on cheese,
they keep it in containers
which they bind about their knees,
they often chew on Cheddar
which they slice into a dish,
and gorge on Gorgonzola
to the wonder of the fish.

The Underwater Wibbles
wiggle blithely through the sea,
munching merrily on Muenster,
grated Feta, bits of Brie,
passing porpoises seem puzzled,
stolid octopuses stare,
as the Wibbles nibble Gouda,
Provolone, Camembert.

The Underwater Wibbles
frolic gaily off the coast,
eating melted Mozzarella
served on soggy crusts of toast,
Wibbles gobble Appenzeller
as they execute their dives,
oh, the Underwater Wibbles
live extraordinary lives.

Jack Prelutsky

The Sliver-Slurk

Down beneath the frogspawn,
Down beneath the reeds,
Down beneath the river's shimmer,
Down beneath the weeds,
Down in dirty darkness,
Down in muddy murk,
Down amongst the sludgy shadows
Lives the Sliver-slurk;

Lives the Sliver-slurk
And the Sliver-slurk's a thing
With a gnawing kind of nibble
And a clammy kind of cling,
With a row of warts on top
And a row of warts beneath
And a horrid way of bubbling through
Its green and stumpy teeth;

With its green and stumpy teeth,
Oh, the Sliver-slurk's a beast
That you'd never find invited
To a party or a feast —
It would terrify the guests,
Make them shake and shout and scream,
Crying: 'Save us from this loathsomeness,
This monster from a dream!'

It's a monster from a dream,
Haunting waters grey and grim,
So be careful where you paddle
Or go happily to swim:
It is down there, it is waiting,
It's a nasty piece of work
And you might just put your foot upon
The slimy Sliver-slurk.

Richard Edwards

Be Wary of the Werewolf Wild

Be wary of the werewolf wild,
he's very big and hairy.
His favourite meal's a little child.
His favourite mode is scary.

His claws are black and sharp and long.
His eyes are gruesome red.
His teeth are yellow, sharp and strong.
He howls when we're in bed.

At dead of night he starts to creep,
and prowl in pale moonlight.
Is there a child not yet asleep?
He's feeling like a bite.

So go to bed and go to sleep
as soon as you are able
or you will be in trouble deep
in a dish on a werewolf's table.

Michaela Morgan

The Glamdrak

Over the hill the Glamdrak came,
its claws were large,
its eyes aflame.

Across the fields the Glamdrak strode,
straddled the fence,
and stood on the road.

Into the town the Glamdrak walked,
with poisoned breath
its quarry it stalked.

In the square the Glamdrak paused,
and screeched its fury
at all the locked doors.

Past the church the Glamdrak went,
into the distance,
its anger spent.

Robin Mellor

Three of a Kind

I stalk the timberland,
I wreck and splinter through,
I smash log cabins,
I wrestle grizzly bears.
At lunch-time if I'm dry
I drain a lake or two,
I send the wolves and wolverines
Howling to their lairs.
I'm Sasquatch,
Bigfoot,
Call me what you like,
But if you're a backpacker
On a forest hike,
Keep a watch behind you,
I'm there, though rarely seen.
I'm Bigfoot,
Sasquatch,
I'm mean, mean, mean.

I pad across the snow field,
Silent as a thief,
The phantom of the blizzard,
Vanishy, rare.
I haunt the barren glacier
And men in disbelief
Goggle at the footprints
I scatter here and there.
I'm Abominable,
Yeti,
Call me what you choose,
But if you're a mountaineer,
Careful when you snooze,
I'm the restless roaming spirit
Of the Himalayan Range.
I'm Yeti,
Abominable,
I'm strange, strange, strange.

I rear up from the waves,
I thresh, I wallow,
My seven snaky humps
Leave an eerie wake.
I crunch the silly salmon,
Twenty at onc swallow,
I tease the silly snoopers —
A fiend? A fish? A fake?
I'm The Monster,
Nessie,
Call me what you please,
But if you're a camper
In the lochside trees,
Before you zip your tent at night
Say your prayers and kneel.
I'm Nessie,
The Monster,
I'm real, real, real.

Richard Edwards

The Truth about the Abominable Footprint

The Yeti's a Beast
Who lives in the East
    And suffers a lot from B.O.
His hot hairy feet
Stink out the street
    So he cools them off in the snow.

Michael Baldwin

The Snow Monster

When the Snow Monster sneezes,
Flurries of snow swirl and whirl,
Twisting round trees, curling into crevices,
Brushing the ground a brilliant white.

When the Snow Monster bellows,
Blizzards blot out the sky,
Piling up drifts, blocking roads,
Burying the landscape in a white grave.

When the Snow Monster cries,
Soft flakes slip and slide gently down
Into the hands of waiting children
Who test their taste with their tongues.

When the Snow Monster sleeps,
The air crackles with children's laughter
As they throw snowballs, build snowmen
And whizz downhill on their sledges.

John Foster

The Fire Monster

Deep in the boiling belly
Of the volcano
The Fire Monster sleeps:
Wisps of smoke from his nostrils
Squeeze through cracks
In the crater's mouth.

Deep in the boiling belly
Of the volcano
The Fire Monster stirs:
Bubbles of lava from his lips
Foam through crevices
And simmer beneath the surface.

Deep in the boiling belly
Of the volcano
The Fire Monster wakes:
Jets of lava gush from his throat,
Squirting through fissures,
Bursting the crater's dam.

Deep in the boiling belly
Of the volcano
The Fire Monster roars:
Huge chunks of rock spit from his mouth.
Red torrents of lava shoot into the sky,
Then stream down the crater's sides.

In the village in the valley,
The watchers wait
For the Fire Monster's anger to abate.

John Foster

The Last Monster

We are the people marching together
With drums loud as thunder and swords at our sides,
Through forests and deserts and cruel grey weather
To the cave in the rocks where the last monster hides.
We are the people marching together
To challenge the terrible beast in its den,
To catch it, to drag it back home on a tether
So children need never fear monsters again.
We are the people marching.

I am the last monster, waiting and weary,
Shivering all day in the chill from the ground,
Life's not worth living now, everything's dreary,
Cramped in this cave as the fog swirls around.
I am the last monster, waiting and weary,
Once I was furious, fearsome and bold,
Once my eyes glittered, but now they're all bleary,
Nothing's so sad as a monster grown old.
I am the last monster, waiting.

Richard Edwards